# CHILES

# CHILES

### W. PARK KERR

William Morrow and Company, Inc.

New York

A hot thank you to Harriet Bell, editor; Louise Fili, designer; Sally Schneider, food styling; Betty Alfenito, prop styling; Ellen Silverman, photographer; Janice Faber and Virginia Mayo, assistants

To Lisa McAlmon, the best friend a guy could ever have

Library of Congress Cataloging-in-Publication Data: Kerr, W. Park. Chiles/by W. Park Kerr. p.cm. ISBN 0-688-13251-0. 1. Cookery (Peppers) 2. Peppers. I. Title. TX803. P46K47 1996 641.6'384 —dc20 95-19031 CIP Printed in the USA. First Edition 1 2 3 4 5 6 7 8 9 10 Design Assistant: Tonya Hudson Book Design: Louise Fili Ltd.

# Introduction

**B**OY, HOW TIMES HAVE CHANGED! EL PASO CHILE COMPANY STARTED ABOUT FIFTEEN YEARS AGO with the chief executive officer (me) standing on street corners selling strings of dried hot chiles. Most of the people who bought them at the time didn't know what to do with them. I saw more than one lady toss the strand of chiles over her head, and confidently walk away the proud owner of a chile necklace.

Now, even local supermarkets are chile-friendly. You'll have no trouble finding pickled jalapeños to sprinkle on your nachos, or canned green chiles, when you can't find good fresh ones, which shouldn't be a problem as produce sections surely carry fresh jalapeños or serranos. And often unfamiliar chiles unexpectedly appear on the produce shelves. One day you may find moderately hot, dark forest green poblanos, and a couple of weeks later there may be a delivery of brilliantly colored, hotter-than-hell habaneros. The chile explosion is not limited to the fresh varieties. Perhaps you've seen unblended powdered chiles, which differ from the ubiquitous chili powders that include cumin and other ingredients, or canned smoked chipotle chiles in a spicy adobo sauce. Dried chiles are also vying for attention from the relatively mild New Mexican varieties (the very kind I sold from street corners) to sweet/hot anchos and tongue-tingling mulattos and cascabels.

While these chiles all share the same genus, *Capsicum,* they have different flavors and heat intensities. Some recipes are just better when prepared with a certain chile type (there are more than two hundred varieties), and each recipe in this book was developed with a particular chile in mind. (See How to Pinch-hit for Your Chiles: Substituting Chile Types on page 32.) It is a common mistake to substitute one kind of chile for another and accidentally create a dish that is too spicy to eat. Confusion has surrounded chiles ever since Columbus came upon them during one of his explorations of the Western hemisphere. Black pepper (a different plant entirely) was one of the things Columbus expected to find in his search to discover a new trade route to the spice-laden East. When he was served spicy food, he assumed it was seasoned with pepper when it was actually sprinkled with ground chiles. To this day, we automatically and incorrectly call some chiles "peppers," such as cayenne pepper.

Chiles traveled quickly all over the world, finding culinary fans in such unexpected, faraway places as China and India. Other than humans, birds are the only other species that will eat chiles willingly. Chile plants developed the spicy fruits to discourage birds from eating the seeds encased within, but the determined birds simply cultivated a resistance to the hotness. In turn, the chile seeds inside the birds protected them—if you were a wolf and chomped on an unexpectedly habanero-flavored sparrow, you'd probably think twice about pouncing on the same type of bird the next time.

But if one looks at the chemical makeup of chiles, their popularity with humans isn't a surprise at all. Chiles combine pleasure and pain in a unique edible package. When we chow down on chiles, we ingest capsaicin, a fiery alkaloid that gives chiles their heat. This substance stimulates salivation and increases perspiration (to cool off the skin in warm climates), all the while causing the brain to release endorphins, chemicals that calm the body and send the message that while the mouth may be tingling with pain, the discomfort will soon pass.

With chiles' heady profile, no wonder salsa has surpassed ketchup as the most popular condiment in America. This book celebrates chiles in all their eye-opening, tongue-teasing, brow-wiping glory.

# Kitchen Cinco Five-Chile Salsa

MAKES ABOUT 2 ½ CUPS

**T**HIS "EVERYTHING BUT THE KITCHEN SINK" SALSA GETS ITS RUDDY COLOR AND TOASTED FLAVOR from four different types of dried chiles, as well as a fresh jalapeño for good measure. You know what to do with salsa…about the only thing it doesn't improve is dessert!

2 large dried red New Mexico chile pods
2 medium anchos
1 medium mulatto
1 medium cascabel
2 cups boiling water
2 medium tomatoes (about 1 pound total)
½ cup chopped yellow onions
3 tablespoons fresh lime juice

3 tablespoons Hot and Cold Tequila
   (page 16) or any good-quality
   unflavored tequila
3 garlic cloves, peeled and chopped
1 ½ medium fresh jalapeños,
   preferably red-ripe, stemmed and chopped
¾ teaspoon salt
⅓ cup finely chopped cilantro

Set a large heavy skillet over medium heat. Arrange the New Mexico, ancho, mulatto, and cascabel chiles in a single layer in the skillet and toast them, turning them occasionally, until they are fragrant and have softened but are not colored or burned, about 4 minutes. Remove the chiles from the skillet, stem and seed them, and tear them into small pieces. In a heat-proof bowl, combine the chile pieces and the boiling water and let stand, covered, stirring once or twice, until cool.

Preheat the broiler. On a broiler-proof pan, cook the tomatoes, turning them once, until the peels are blackened, about 20 minutes total. Remove from the broiler and cool to room temperature. Core the tomatoes.

Drain the chiles, reserving 3 tablespoons of the soaking water. In a food processor, combine the tomatoes, their burned peels and any juices, the chiles, reserved soaking water, onions, lime juice, tequila, garlic, jalapeños, and salt and process until smooth. Cover and refrigerate for at least 30 minutes and preferably overnight. Bring the salsa to room temperature. Stir in the cilantro, adjust the seasoning, and serve.

# Picking Peppers: Buying Chiles

**M**ORE AND MORE SUPERMARKETS ARE CARRYING A WIDE CHOICE OF FRESH CHILES, BUT NO MATTER WHAT TYPE, the same purchasing rules apply. Fresh chiles should be shiny and firm, without any soft spots. (Some chiles have thin, wrinkle-like markings, which are not a sign of age.) Red chiles are fully ripe, so they have a sweeter, rounder taste than the less ripe green ones, and they are also more perishable. Store fresh chiles in a single layer on a paper towel–lined plate or pan in the refrigerator, loosely covered, as they mold more easily in plastic bags. If good and fresh, they will keep for about one week.

Freezing is one of the best ways to preserve fresh chiles. The chiles must be fire-roasted (page 11), as unroasted fresh chiles don't freeze well. After fire-roasting, cool the chiles, leaving them unpeeled. Place about six or so into plastic freezer bags, and freeze for up to six months. Thaw and peel the chiles before using.

Dried chiles, powdered chiles, and chili powders (which are ground chile peppers seasoned with other spices as a flavoring for a pot of chili) should be bought from a source that has a quick turnover of these items—their flavor fades with time. Insects love chiles, so if you live in a humid climate that has lots of little critters in the summer, store the tightly wrapped chiles in the refrigerator. If you don't plan to use your stash of dried chiles within a year, freeze them for storage. Otherwise, keep them in airtight containers (glass canning jars are perfect) in a cool, dry spot.

*Ristras,* those colorful strings of dried chiles for sale all over the Southwest, are traditionally calculated to last just long enough for next year's crop to be turning red in the fields. If you buy a *ristra,* watch out: don't buy the ones preserved with shellac if you plan to cook with the chiles. Can you believe that there are people who use *ristras* only for decoration and not for cooking? Nothing ruins a bowl of chili quicker than a mouthful of shellacked chiles!

# Take It Off: Roasting and Peeling Fresh Chiles

FRESH CHILES HAVE A TOUGH, INDIGESTIBLE PEEL THAT SHOULD BE DISCARDED BEFORE USING, and the easiest way to remove it is by fire-roasting. This procedure also partially cooks the flesh as it adds a smoky flavor. If you have a gas range, you can place the chiles right on the burner grids and cook them over a medium flame, adjusting the flame so it doesn't lick around the chiles. To roast a lot of fresh chiles, light up the charcoal grill and do them outside. With an electric stove, prepare the chiles on a stovetop grill or char them under the broiler. (Broiled chiles will be softer than the gas burner–roasted ones, but still fine.)

No matter what method you choose, first pierce the chiles near the stem end with the tip of a knife. People with tender skin will probably prefer to always wear rubber gloves when handling chiles to avoid getting the irritating oils on their skin, and all cooks should avoid touching their eyes or other delicate parts of the body after chile preparation. Roast or broil the chiles, turning them often, until the peels are lightly but evenly charred. Do not roast the chiles so long that you burn a hole through the flesh or white ash forms—remember, you are only *charring* the peels. Place the chiles in a paper bag or bowl and close or cover tightly. Let stand and steam until cool enough to handle, about 15 minutes. Using a paper towel or rubber gloves, rub away as much of the charred peel as possible. If there are a few stubborn spots, try scraping off the peel with a small knife, but don't worry about it too much—a little burned peel won't hurt. Don't rinse the chiles, as plenty of flavor will go down the drain. Remove the stems, trim away the ribs and seeds, and cut up the chiles as the recipe directs.

# Freezing Roasted Chiles

**F**REEZING IS ONE OF THE BEST WAYS TO PRESERVE THE FLEET-ING, SEASONAL PERFECTION OF FIELD-RIPENED FRESH CHILES. After fire-roasting (page 11), the chiles are merely cooled, not peeled, and packed, six or so at a time, into plastic freezer bags. Thaw and peel the chiles before using.

# Heatin' Up: Toasting Dried Chiles

**T**HE TOASTING OF DRIED CHILE PEPPERS IS OPTIONAL. TOASTING MAKES CHILES MORE FLEXIBLE and easier to stem and seed, and adds a smoky nuance that will enrich the flavor of a finished dish.

It's easy to do. For chiles, set a large heavy skillet or griddle over medium heat. Place the chiles in the skillet in a single layer. Turning occasionally, cook the chiles until flexible, fragrant, and just lightly colored; this will take no more than 4 to 5 minutes. The chiles should not become dark, brittle, or burned, or they will be bitter. Immediately remove the chiles from the skillet (they will continue to cook, and possibly scorch, if allowed to stand in the hot utensil) and stem and seed them while still warm. Chiles store their spiciness in the ribs and seeds, so save the seeds to sprinkle in a dish if you feel it could be seasoned with more heat. Those little guys are hot!

# Crunchy Sweet and Spicy Chile Pecans

MAKES ABOUT 3 CUPS

**T**HESE CRUNCHY LITTLE DEVILS ARE SO ADDICTIVE, I SOME-TIMES THINK THEY SHOULD COME WITH A PRESCRIPTION for refills. Chiles and sugar may sound like an odd match, but remember that chiles are fruits, after all, and the best New Mexican ground chiles (from Chimayo, for example) have an inherent sweet note.

¼ cup sugar

3 tablespoons unblended medium-hot
    powdered red chiles, preferably from
    Chimayo or Dixon, New Mexico

¾ teaspoon salt

½ teaspoon ground cinnamon

½ teaspoon freshly grated nutmeg

¾ pound (about 3 cups) jumbo pecan
    halves

2 egg whites, well beaten

Position a rack in the middle of the oven and preheat to 375°F. Spray a jelly roll pan lightly with nonstick spray.

In a small bowl, thoroughly combine the sugar, powdered chiles, salt, cinnamon, and nutmeg. In a medium bowl, stir together the pecans and egg whites. While the whites are still wet, sprinkle the spice mixture over the pecans while stirring constantly; the nuts should be thoroughly and evenly coated.

Spread the nuts in a single layer on the prepared pan. Bake for 5 minutes. Stir to break up any clumps of nuts. Bake, stirring often, until the nuts are lightly browned and crisp, another 7 to 10 minutes.

Remove from the oven and cool to room temperature. Store at room temperature in an airtight container. The nuts can be kept for up to 1 week, except during humid weather.

# Hot and Cold Tequila

MAKES ABOUT 3 CUPS

**I** KEEP A BOTTLE OF THIS INCREDIBLE CONCOCTION IN THE FREEZER, POISED TO POUR INTO A CHILLED MARTINI GLASS, just in case I have an emergency situation that calls for an attitude adjustment. Try it poured into tomato juice for a breathtaking eye-opener, or drink shots to accompany a platter of chilled shellfish.

1 750-milliliter bottle best-quality silver tequila

2 fresh jalapeños (1 red and 1 green if available), stemmed and quartered

1 green onion, trimmed to fit the tequila bottle

1 fresh serrano, stemmed and quartered

1 chile de árbol, stemmed, split, and seeded

1 medium garlic clove, peeled and halved

Zest (colored peel) of 1 lime or ½ orange, removed in a long, thin strip

Pour off about ½ cup of the tequila and reserve it for another use.

Drop the jalapeños, green onion, serrano, chile de árbol, garlic clove halves, and lime zest into the bottle. Cover and let stand at room temperature for 48 hours.

Store the bottle in the freezer. The tequila will become thick and syrupy. Serve directly from the freezer.

# Little Tostadas of Salmon Ceviche with Serranos

**H**AVING A FANCY PARTY WHERE YOU WANT SUPER-ELEGANT HORS D'OEUVRES TO PASS WITH DRINKS? Look no further than these crunchy little tortilla rounds topped with lime-and-tequila marinated salmon cubes. For a main course, arrange the topping ingredients over four fried 6-inch tortillas instead of the tostaditas.

12 6-inch corn tortillas

2 cups corn oil

1 teaspoon salt

1 ½ pounds boneless, skinless fresh
   salmon, cut into ½-inch cubes

1 ¼ cups fresh lime juice

½ cup diced red onions

4 fresh serranos, stemmed and cut into
   very thin rounds

3 tablespoons minced cilantro

2 tablespoons Hot and Cold Tequila
   (page 16) or any good-quality
   unflavored tequila

2 tablespoons olive oil

½ teaspoon salt

2 cups shredded romaine lettuce

1 large just-ripe mango, pitted, peeled,
   and cut into ½-inch cubes

Using a 2 ½-inch cookie cutter, cut out 24 rounds of tortillas. In a large skillet over medium heat, warm the oil. Working in batches, add the tortilla rounds and fry, turning once or twice, until crisp, about 2 minutes. With a slotted spoon, transfer the rounds to paper towels. Sprinkle lightly with salt to taste. *(The tortilla rounds can be fried up to 1 day ahead. Wrap airtight and store at room temperature. Rewarm in a 200°F oven for about 5 minutes before using, if desired.)*

In a medium bowl, combine the salmon and lime juice. Cover and refrigerate, stirring occasionally, until the cubes of fish are firm yet remain slightly uncooked at their centers, about 3 hours. Drain the salmon, reserving 2 tablespoons of the lime juice.

In a medium bowl, gently toss together the fish, onions, serranos, cilantro, reserved lime juice, tequila, olive oil, and salt. Arrange the tortilla rounds on a large platter. Divide the shredded lettuce among the tortilla rounds. Top the lettuce with the ceviche, dividing it evenly and using it all. Drizzle each tostada with some of the liquid remaining in the bowl. Scatter the diced mango over the tostadas and serve immediately.

# Red Chili Purée

MAKES ABOUT 2 CUPS

RED CHILE PURÉE, CREATED FROM REHYDRATED DRIED CHILES, IS RARELY SERVED STRAIGHT AS A SAUCE but is used as an ingredient in a recipe. Dried New Mexico chiles vary in hotness, so be sure you are buying the intensity you want.

6 cups boiling water

¼ pound (about 12 large) mild New Mexico red chile pods, stemmed, seeded, and torn into small pieces

2 chiles de árbol, stemmed and torn into small pieces

1 cup hot tap water

In a medium heat-proof bowl, combine the boiling water with the pieces of chile. Cover and let stand, stirring occasionally, until cool.

Drain, discarding the soaking water. In a food processor, combine the soaked chile pieces with the hot tap water and process, stopping to scrape down the sides of the work bowl once or twice, until smooth.

Transfer the purée to a sieve set over a bowl. With a rubber scraper, force the purée through the sieve into the bowl; discard any tough peels or seeds that remain. *(The purée can be covered and refrigerated for up to 3 days or frozen for up to 2 months.)*

# Red Chili Gravy

**O**NCE YOU HAVE MADE RED CHILE PURÉE (PAGE 21), YOU CAN TURN IT INTO RED CHILE GRAVY, which can then be used to sauce enchiladas, huevos rancheros, or any number of fabulous foods. This is the Real Thing, as far away from insipid canned enchilada sauce as you can get… and that's a good thing.

3 tablespoons olive oil

½ cup minced yellow onions

3 garlic cloves, peeled and minced

1 teaspoon ground cumin, preferably from toasted seeds (page 32)

½ teaspoon dried oregano, crumbled

½ teaspoon dried marjoram, crumbled

2 tablespoons unbleached all-purpose flour

4 cups (2 recipes) Red Chile Purée (page 21)

1 ¾ cups lightly salted chicken broth

1 ½ teaspoons salt

1 ½ teaspoons cider vinegar

¾ teaspoon packed light brown sugar

In a medium saucepan over low heat, warm the olive oil. Add the onions, garlic, cumin, oregano, and marjoram and cook, uncovered, stirring once or twice, for 5 minutes. Whisk in the flour and cook, stirring and mashing the flour mixture, for 2 minutes. Whisk in the chile purée, chicken broth, salt, cider vinegar, and brown sugar. Bring to a simmer, then lower the heat and cook, partially covered, stirring often, until the sauce has thickened to a medium consistency, about 20 minutes. (*The sauce can be cooled completely, covered tightly, and refrigerated for up to 3 days or frozen for up to 2 months. Bring to room temperature before using.*)

# Green Chile Sauce

MAKES ABOUT 4 CUPS

THE VERY ESSENCE OF GREEN CHILES, THIS ELEMENTAL SAUCE IS AS IMPORTANT TO SOUTHWESTERN COOKING as a well-made tomato sauce is to Italian cuisine. It is spooned over eggs, Tex-Mex tortilla-based dishes, grilled meats and fish—you name it. If you have asbestos taste buds, you can add a minced jalapeño or two, but I prepare it only mildly hot for the most versatility.

2 tablespoons olive oil
1/2 cup finely chopped yellow onions
2 garlic cloves, peeled and minced
1/2 teaspoon dried oregano, crumbled
1/4 teaspoon ground cumin, preferably
   from toasted seeds (page 32)
3 tablespoons unbleached all-purpose flour

1 cup lightly salted chicken broth
1 cup water
12 long green chiles, roasted, peeled,
   and chopped (page 11), or 2 cups
   frozen chopped green chiles,
   thawed and drained
3/4 teaspoon salt

In a medium heavy saucepan over low heat, warm the olive oil. Add the onions, garlic, oregano, and cumin; cover and cook, stirring once or twice, for 8 minutes. Uncover, stir in the flour, and cook, stirring often, for 2 minutes. Stir in the chicken broth, water, green chiles, and salt and bring to a simmer. Cook, uncovered, stirring occasionally, until thick, about 15 minutes. *(The sauce can be prepared ahead. Cool completely, cover, and refrigerate for up to 3 days or freeze for up to 1 month.)*

# Sweet Red Pepper Soup with Jalapeño Croutons

**H**OT OR COLD, THIS GORGEOUS SOUP LOOKS AND TASTES SPEC-TACULAR. It gives the impression of being sinfully rich, and your guests will be surprised when they find out it isn't loaded with cream.

½ stick (4 tablespoons) unsalted butter

2 cups chopped leeks

1 cup chopped yellow onions

2 tablespoons sweet Hungarian paprika

1 teaspoon ground cumin, preferably from toasted seeds (page 32)

1 teaspoon dried basil, crumbled

3 bay leaves

3 pounds sweet red peppers, stemmed, seeded, and coarsely chopped

5 cups lightly salted chicken broth

1 teaspoon salt

Jalapeño Croutons (recipe follows)

In a 5-quart soup pot over medium heat, melt the butter. Add the leeks, onions, paprika, cumin, basil, and bay leaves; cover and cook, stirring occasionally, for 10 minutes. Add the sweet peppers; cover and cook, stirring occasionally, for 10 minutes. Add the chicken broth and salt and bring to a simmer. Partially cover the pan and cook, stirring occasionally, until the peppers are very tender, about 35 minutes.

Cool slightly, then force the soup through the medium blade of a soup mill. (The soup can be prepared to this point up to 3 days ahead and can be served hot or cold. Cool completely, cover, and refrigerate.) Rewarm the soup over low heat if you are serving it hot. Adjust seasoning. Ladle the soup into bowls. Sprinkle the croutons over the soup and serve immediately.

## Jalapeño Croutons

2 tablespoons unsalted butter

2 tablespoons olive oil

3 whole garlic cloves, peeled

2 fresh jalapeños, stemmed and quartered

2 cups firm white peasant-style sourdough bread, cut into ½-inch cubes

Salt

In a large skillet over medium heat, melt the butter in the olive oil. Add the garlic cloves and jalapeños and cook, stirring often without browning, for 7 minutes. With a slotted spoon, remove the garlic cloves and chiles and discard. Add the bread cubes to the skillet, tossing to coat them evenly with the oil. Cook, stirring occasionally, until the cubes are lightly but evenly browned, about 7 minutes. Season with salt and use warm.

# Jalapeño Risotto with Sonoma Dry Jack Cheese

MAKES 6 SERVINGS

YOU CAN REALLY TASTE THE JALAPEÑOS IN THIS TONGUE-TINGLING RISOTTO, but tender tongues may want to use fewer peppers. Sonoma Dry Jack is an aged Parmesan-like cheese from California (Williams-Sonoma often carries it by mail order), and Italian Parmigiano-Reggiano can be substituted. But there is no substitute for arborio rice, which possesses the special creamy quality that defines a fine risotto.

6 cups lightly salted chicken broth
1 stick (8 tablespoons) unsalted butter
1 cup finely chopped yellow onions
6 medium fresh jalapeños, stems, ribs, and seeds removed, finely diced

1 garlic clove, peeled and minced
1 1/2 cups arborio rice
1/4 pound Vella Sonoma Dry Jack cheese, grated

In a medium saucepan, bring the broth to a simmer.

In a large heavy saucepan over low heat, melt the butter. Stir in the onions, jalapeños, and garlic and cook, stirring once or twice, for 5 minutes. Add the rice, stir to coat well with the butter, and cook 2 minutes. Stir in 1 cup of the hot broth. Cook, stirring frequently, until the rice absorbs almost all the broth, about 5 minutes. Continue adding broth 1 cup at a time and stirring often between additions, until the rice has absorbed most of the broth and is tender and creamy, about 30 minutes total.

Stir 1/3 cup of the grated cheese into the risotto, cover, and let stand 1 minute. Divide the risotto evenly between 6 plates and serve immediately, passing the remaining cheese and a peppermill at the table.

# Red River Valley Barbecue Sauce

MAKES ABOUT 3 ¾ CUPS

**I** HAVE SIMMERED UP A LOT OF BARBECUE SAUCE, BUT DON'T ASK ME WHICH ONE I LIKE BEST. That said, this is absolutely the best dipping and glazing sauce in creation, and if you use it on your barbecue, the world will kneel before you at your grill.

⅓ cup corn oil

½ cup finely chopped yellow onions

2 garlic cloves, peeled and minced

3 tablespoons unblended medium-hot powdered red chiles, preferably from Chimayo or Dixon, New Mexico

1 tablespoon dry mustard

1 ¼ teaspoons dried thyme, crumbled

1 ¼ teaspoons ground ginger

1 teaspoon ground cumin, preferably from toasted seeds (page 32)

1 teaspoon freshly ground black pepper

¾ teaspoon crushed hot red pepper flakes

2 bay leaves

1 ¾ cups ketchup

1 cup fresh orange juice

¼ cup fresh lemon juice

¼ cup unsulfured molasses

2 tablespoons Worcestershire sauce

2 tablespoons soy sauce

1 teaspoon hot pepper sauce

In a medium, heavy, preferably nonstick saucepan over low heat, warm the oil. Add the onions, garlic, powdered chiles, mustard, thyme, ginger, cumin, black pepper, crushed red pepper, and bay leaves. Cover and cook, stirring occasionally, for 10 minutes. Add the ketchup, orange juice, lemon juice, molasses, Worcestershire sauce, soy sauce, and hot pepper sauce and bring to a simmer. Cook, uncovered, stirring often as the sauce begins to thicken, for 20 minutes.

Remove from the heat and refrigerate for at least 24 hours to allow the flavors to mellow. Bring to room temperature and discard the bay leaves before using.

# Café Centrál's "Tromped-On" Marinated Jalapeños

**A**T EL PASO'S CAFÉ CENTRÁL, JALAPEÑO PEPPERS ARE FIRST DEEP-FRIED (which collapses them, providing their weird name), then soaked for a long spell in soy and Worcestershire sauces and served as a garnish to grilled meats.

*Peanut oil, for deep-frying*      *½ cup soy sauce*
*1 pound small or medium fresh jalapeños*      *½ cup Worcestershire sauce*

In a deep heavy saucepan fitted with a frying thermometer and set over medium heat, or in an electric deep-fryer, warm about 4 inches of oil to 375°F. (The pan or fryer should be no more than half full.)

Working in small batches, lower the jalapeños into the hot oil (it will boil vigorously) and cook, turning the chiles often, until they are wrinkled and brown, 4 to 5 minutes. With a slotted spoon, transfer the jalapeños to a medium bowl.

Pour the soy sauce and Worcestershire sauce over the jalapeños and cool to room temperature. Cover and refrigerate, stirring gently once or twice, for at least 1 week before eating. The chiles will keep for up to 1 month.

# Sherry-Serrano Table Shake

**S**O, YOU WANT A SPLASH OF HOT PEPPER SAUCE FOR YOUR SCRAMBLED EGGS OR WHATEVER. You could use a bottle of store-bought stuff (varying greatly in intensity from brand to brand, by the way), or you could proudly pull out this fabulous homemade version, concocted with Spanish sherry vinegar and lots of fresh chiles.

¼ pound fresh serranos, ideally a mixture
   of green and red-ripe
1 cup imported sherry vinegar

1 tablespoon packed light brown sugar
1 tablespoon soy sauce

Stem the serranos and cut them in half lengthwise. There should be about 1 cup. In a 2-cup nonreactive container (a glass bottle with a shaker top is ideal), combine the serranos, vinegar, sugar, and soy sauce and shake to dissolve the sugar. Cover the bottle and let stand at room temperature for 48 hours before using. Store in the refrigerator.

# How to Pinch-hit for Your Chiles: Substituting Chile Types

SOME SUPERMARKETS NOW HAVE SO MANY CHILE PEPPER VARI-ETIES YOU MIGHT THINK YOU ARE AT A MEXICAN *MERCADO*. At others you are lucky if they carry a few jalapeños hidden away in a corner of the produce section. At some time or another, most chile lovers will be forced to substitute one type of pepper for another, and unfortunately, the results will be variable.

For example, two of the most popular chiles, jalapeño and serrano, are close enough in flavor that two of the small serranos could easily stand in for one jalapeño. As heat level always varies from variety to variety, substitute by taste, not by volume. If you minced 1 tablespoon of the highly incendiary tiny Thai bird peppers to use for 1 table-spoon of jalapeño, you would have one hell of a hot dish. (There is one interesting rule of thumb: the smaller the chile variety, the hotter it often is.) Canned green chiles are rec-ommended only as a last resort, but they are better than no chiles at all. These now come in mild, medium, and hot varieties, so it is best to add them by taste, not volume, as well.

Two particular chiles, the Caribbean habanero and the Mexican chipotle (available dried or canned in a spicy sauce), have very distinctive flavors that are hard to duplicate. The bonnet-shaped habanero should come with a warning label, as it is about twenty times hotter than a jalapeño, but for all its heat, it has a definite vegetable taste. Chipotles are also fiery, but they are smoked too, making substitution even more difficult.

Chile aficionados know that each chile is an individual, with a strong personality, and they feel that substituting does a disservice to their diversity. But not everyone lives near a source for great chiles. Use the mail order sources (page 60) to stock yourself with chiles or chile seeds for the garden, and whenever hard-to-find fresh chiles appear in your market, react with trigger-finger quickness and cook them up accordingly.

## Toasting Cumin

TO AVOID OVERBROWNING THE CUMIN (AND DESTROYING THE SOUGHT-AFTER NUTTY TASTE), begin with a generous quantity of seeds—half a cup or so. Set the seeds in a small heavy skillet over low heat and cook, stirring often, until browned and fragrant (some seeds may pop), 7 to 8 minutes. Remove from the skillet immediately and cool. Store the toasted seeds airtight with other spices and grind them when needed in an electric spice mill or in a mortar with a pestle.

# Island Chicken and Fruit Kabobs with Jalapeño-Peanut Sauce

**T**HERE SEEMS TO BE AN EQUATION OF THE HOTTER THE CLIMATE, THE HOTTER THE FOOD. Many tropical islands make a marinated skewered chicken, typically served with a peanutty coconut-milk dip like Jalapeño-Peanut Sauce.

¼ cup fresh lime juice

¼ cup Myers's Original dark rum

1-inch cube peeled fresh ginger, chopped

3 tablespoons packed dark brown sugar

2 tablespoons Pickapeppa sauce

3 garlic cloves, peeled and chopped

1 tablespoon soy sauce

½ teaspoon ground allspice

3 pounds boneless, skinless chicken breasts, trimmed, pounded flat, and cut lengthwise into 1-inch-wide strips

1 medium-large pineapple (about 3 pounds), peeled, cored, and cut into 1-inch chunks

3 just-ripe, still-firm bananas, peeled and cut into 1-inch chunks

2 cups wood smoking chips, soaked in water for at least 30 minutes

Jalapeño-Peanut Sauce (recipe follows), warmed

½ cup grated fresh coconut or unsweetened dried coconut (available in health food stores)

In a mini food processor or blender, combine the lime juice, rum, ginger, brown sugar, Pickapeppa, garlic, soy sauce, and allspice and purée until smooth. In a shallow nonreactive dish, combine the purée and strips of chicken. Cover and marinate at room temperature, stirring once or twice, for no more than 1 hour.

Remove the chicken strips from the marinade, reserving the marinade. Fold the chicken strips by thirds onto themselves to form compact bundles. Evenly divide the chicken bundles, pineapple chunks, and banana chunks and thread onto 6 flat metal skewers, alternating them and using them all.

Light a charcoal fire and let it burn down until the coals are evenly white or preheat a gas grill (medium-high). Drain the wood chips and scatter them over the hot coals or lava stones. Position the rack about 6 inches above the heat source.

When the wood chips are smoking, lay the skewers on the grill. Cover and cook, basting the chicken and fruit chunks with the reserved marinade and turning the skewers

once or twice, until the chicken is just cooked through and is lightly browned, about 8 minutes total. Remove the skewers from the grill.

Spoon a generous pool of peanut sauce onto each of 6 plates. Lay the skewers over the peanut sauce (or slide the chicken and fruit off the skewers onto the sauce), sprinkle with coconut, and serve immediately.

### Jalapeño-Peanut Sauce

2 jalapeños, roasted (page 11) and stemmed

1/4-inch slice fresh ginger (about 1 inch diameter), peeled

3 tablespoons fresh lime juice

3 tablespoons molasses

2 tablespoons Myers's Original dark rum

2 garlic cloves, peeled and chopped

1 teaspoon soy sauce

1 cup canned coconut milk (not coconut cream), available in specialty food shops and some supermarkets

1 cup lightly salted chicken broth

3/4 cup supermarket-type (not "natural") chunky peanut butter

2 teaspoons curry powder

In a mini food processor or blender, combine the jalapeños, ginger, lime juice, molasses, rum, garlic, and soy sauce and process until smooth.

In a medium nonreactive saucepan over low heat, combine the jalapeño mixture, coconut milk, chicken broth, peanut butter, and curry powder. Cook, stirring often, until the sauce just reaches a simmer. Remove from the heat; use hot or warm.

# Grilled Cilantro Swordfish with Green Pumpkin Seed Salsa

MAKES 8 SERVINGS

**F**OR EXTRA-SASSY SWORDFISH STEAKS, MAKE THIS WITH HOT AND COLD TEQUILA. Don't think that marinating the fish longer than 1 hour will make it better—the acids in the lime juice will "cook" the swordfish and make it tough.

1/3 cup fresh lime juice

1/3 cup Hot and Cold Tequila (page 16) or any good-quality unflavored tequila

1/3 cup olive oil

1/3 cup chopped cilantro

2 garlic cloves, crushed

1 teaspoon freshly ground black pepper

8 1 1/2-inch-thick swordfish steaks (about 5 pounds total)

2 cups wood smoking chips, preferably mesquite, soaked in water for at least 30 minutes

Salt

Green Pumpkin Seed Salsa (recipe follows)

In a small bowl, whisk together the lime juice, tequila, olive oil, cilantro, garlic, and pepper. Lay the swordfish steaks in a shallow nonreactive dish just large enough to hold them. Pour the lime juice mixture over the fish; cover and marinate at room temperature, turning once or twice, for 1 hour.

Light a charcoal fire and let it burn down until the coals are evenly white or preheat a gas grill (medium). Drain the wood chips and scatter them over the hot coals or lava stones. Position the rack about 6 inches above the heat source.

When the chips are smoking heavily, remove the fish steaks from the marinade (reserving the marinade), lay them on the grill rack, and cover. Cook the steaks, turning them once or twice and basting them with marinade, until just cooked through while remaining juicy, 8 to 9 minutes total.

Set the fish steaks on plates. Season lightly with salt, then spread a generous dollop of the salsa next to each steak. Serve immediately.

# Green Pumpkin Seed Salsa

6 medium fresh tomatillos (about 1/3 pound), husked

1 cup raw pumpkin seeds (available in health food stores)

6 long green chiles, roasted, peeled, and chopped (page 11), or 1 cup frozen chopped green chiles, thawed and drained

1 cup chopped watercress

1/2 cup chopped cilantro

1/2 cup chopped yellow onions

1/4 cup lightly salted chicken broth

2 medium fresh jalapeños, roasted (page 11) and stemmed

2 tablespoons fresh lime juice

1 tablespoon balsamic vinegar

1 tablespoon olive oil

1 teaspoon salt

In a shallow pan under a preheated broiler, or on a chile-roasting rack over a medium burner, roast the tomatillos, turning them, until the skins blacken, about 10 minutes under the boiler, 5 to 7 minutes on a burner rack. Remove and cool.

In a large heavy skillet over medium heat, toast the pumpkin seeds, stirring them often, until they are lightly and evenly browned and have popped, about 10 minutes. Remove from the skillet and cool.

In a food processor, combine the roasted tomatillos, pumpkin seeds, green chiles, watercress, cilantro, onions, chicken broth, jalapeños, lime juice, vinegar, olive oil, and salt. Process, stopping to scrape down the sides of the work bowl once or twice, until the salsa is smooth. Adjust the seasoning. (The salsa can be prepared up to 2 days ahead. Cover and refrigerate, returning it to room temperature before using.)

# Poblano Rellenos with Smoky Tomato Sauce

**F**RESH POBLANO CHILES, WITH THEIR INVITINGLY HOLLOW INSIDES, ARE JUST ASKING TO BE FILLED, and I oblige with a Cheddar and goat cheese mixture made chunky with chopped hominy (you can substitute unchopped corn kernels if you wish). Rich and flavorful, they can be served as a first course if the main course is light, perhaps grilled chicken or fish.

4 medium poblanos, roasted and
  peeled (page 11)

2 ounces sharp Cheddar cheese, grated

2 ounces soft, mild goat cheese, at room
  temperature

½ cup drained canned hominy, coarsely
  chopped

2 green onions, tops included, thinly sliced

3 cups peanut or corn oil

3 eggs, at room temperature

1 tablespoon water

3 tablespoons unbleached all-purpose flour

¼ teaspoon salt

Smoky Tomato Sauce (recipe follows),
  heated to simmering

Sprigs of cilantro, for garnish

Cut a vertical slit in one side of each chile and, with a fingertip, scrape out as many seeds as possible without tearing the chile.

In a small bowl, stir together the Cheddar cheese, goat cheese, hominy, and green onions. Stuff one-quarter of the cheese mixture carefully into each chile. Gently press the slits closed.

In a large skillet over medium-high heat, warm the oil to 375°F.

Meanwhile, separate the eggs, transferring the whites to a medium mixing bowl and the yolks to a wide shallow bowl. Whisk the egg yolks and water together. Whisk in the flour and salt. With a clean beater, whip the egg whites to soft peaks. Thoroughly stir one-third of the whites into the yolk mixture. Gently fold in the remaining whites; do not overmix.

Dip a chile into the batter, coating it thoroughly. With a pancake turner, carefully lower the chile, slit side up, into the hot oil. Immediately baste the upper side of the chile with hot oil (this seals the slit and prevents melted cheese from oozing out). Repeat with the remaining chiles.

Cook, turning once, until the batter is crisp and golden, about 5 minutes total. With a slotted spoon transfer the chiles to paper towels; drain briefly.

Spoon the tomato sauce into 4 shallow bowls, dividing it evenly and using it all. Set a chile atop the sauce in each bowl, garnish with cilantro, and serve immediately.

## Smoky Tomato Sauce

2 tablespoons olive oil

½ cup chopped yellow onions

2 garlic cloves, peeled and chopped

½ teaspoon dried oregano, crumbled

½ teaspoon ground cumin, preferably from toasted seeds (page 32)

Generous pinch of ground cinnamon

1 ¼ pounds ripe Italian-style plum tomatoes, trimmed and chunked

½ cup chicken broth

2 canned chipotles en adobo, minced

½ teaspoon salt

In a medium saucepan over low heat, warm the olive oil. Add the onions, garlic, oregano, cumin, and cinnamon and cook, covered, stirring once or twice, until tender, about 7 minutes. Add the tomatoes, broth, chipotles, and salt and bring to a simmer. Partially cover and cook, stirring once or twice, for 20 minutes. Uncover and cook until the tomatoes are very tender and the sauce has thickened slightly, about 10 minutes.

Cool slightly, then pulse the sauce in a food processor or blender. Do not purée. *(The sauce can be prepared up to 3 days ahead. Cover and refrigerate. Reheat before serving.)*

# Marinated Spareribs Chimayo

**N**ORTHERN NEW MEXICO HAS A SHORT, INTENSE GROWING SEASON THAT PRODUCES RED-RIPENED CHILES with a unique sweet-fruity heat. Named, like wines, after the villages near the fields, they are best in simple, straightforward dishes like these oven-braised spareribs in a thick gravy. Allow the spareribs to wallow in the marinade for 24 hours before baking.

2 cups chopped yellow onions

½ cup lightly salted chicken broth

6 tablespoons unblended medium-hot powdered red chiles, preferably from Chimayo or Dixon, New Mexico

4 garlic cloves, peeled and minced

2 tablespoons red wine vinegar

1 teaspoon dried oregano, crumbled

½ teaspoon ground cumin, preferably from toasted seeds (page 32)

½ teaspoon salt

4 ½ pounds country-style pork spareribs

In a food processor, combine the onions, broth, powdered chiles, garlic, vinegar, oregano, cumin, and salt and process to a smooth paste.

In a shallow nonreactive baking dish, arrange the spareribs in a single layer. Spread the chile paste evenly over the ribs; cover and refrigerate, stirring once or twice, for 24 hours. Return the ribs to room temperature.

Position a rack in the middle of the oven and preheat to 350°F. Tightly cover the dish and bake for 30 minutes. Turn the spareribs, re-cover the dish, and bake for 30 minutes. Uncover the dish and bake, basting the ribs with the pan juices and turning them once or twice, until they are very tender and lightly browned, 1 to 1 ¼ hours more.

Transfer the ribs to a platter. Degrease the pan juices, spoon them over the ribs, and serve immediately.

# Grilled Pork Tenderloins with Chipotle-Marmalade Glaze

**G**RILLED PORK TENDERLOINS ARE IRRESISTIBLE WHEN PRE-PARED WITH THIS SWEET, HOT, AND SMOKY GLAZE. This meal comes together quicker than a jackrabbit on a treadmill.

1 cup orange marmalade

3 canned chipotles en adobo, with clinging sauce

2 tablespoons dark Asian sesame oil

2 pork tenderloins (about 1 pound each), tough outer membrane and any fat removed

2 tablespoons sesame seeds

2 cups fruitwood smoking chips, soaked in water for at least 30 minutes

In a mini food processor, combine the marmalade, chipotles, and sesame oil and process until smooth. In a shallow dish, combine the marmalade mixture and pork and let stand, covered, for 30 minutes.

In a small skillet over low heat, toast the sesame seeds, stirring often, until golden, about 5 minutes. Remove from the heat.

Light a charcoal fire and let it burn down until the coals are evenly white or preheat a gas grill (medium). Drain the wood chips and scatter them over the hot coals or lava stones. Set the rack about 6 inches above the heat source.

When the wood chips are smoking heavily, lay the tenderloins on the rack, cover, and cook, turning occasionally, and basting with any glaze remaining in the bowl, until they are crisply glazed and cooked through while remaining slightly pink at their thickest, about 20 minutes.

Cut the tenderloins across the grain and at a slight angle into thin slices. Sprinkle with the toasted sesame seeds and serve hot, warm, or cool.

# Vegetable and Poblano Ragout

**I** AM A CARD-CARRYING CARNIVORE, BUT I DON'T MIND SITTING DOWN TO A BOWL OF THIS HEARTY VEGETABLE STEW one little bit. Served with a hunk of corn bread and a crisp salad, it has made me ponder (briefly, but seriously) the vegetarian life. If you want to serve it to non-meat-eating friends, substitute vegetable broth for the chicken broth.

I *large eggplant (about 1 ¼ pounds),*
   *trimmed, quartered, and cut into*
   *¾-inch slices*
4 *teaspoons salt*
I *pound orange winter squash, such as*
   *butternut, peeled and cut into*
   *¾-inch cubes*
About *½ cup olive oil*

I *medium onion, sliced*
4 *garlic cloves, peeled and minced*
4 *poblanos, roasted, peeled (page 11),*
   *and cut into julienne strips*
2 *cups tender sweet corn kernels and juices,*
   *cut and scraped from 4 medium ears*
I *cup lightly salted chicken broth*
½ *cup julienned fresh basil leaves*

In a colander set over a plate, sprinkle the eggplant slices with about 2 teaspoons of salt. Let stand for 30 minutes.

Bring a medium pan of water to a boil. Stir in the squash cubes and 2 teaspoons salt and cook, uncovered, stirring once or twice, until just tender, about 15 minutes; drain.

Pat the eggplant slices dry. In a large, deep, preferably nonstick skillet over medium heat, warm 1 ½ tablespoons of the olive oil. Working in batches and adding another 1 ½ tablespoons of oil when needed, cook the eggplant slices, turning them once, until well browned, about 3 minutes per side. Transfer the browned eggplant to a bowl.

Add the remaining olive oil to the skillet and set over medium heat. Add the onion, garlic, and poblanos and cook, covered, stirring once or twice, for 10 minutes. Add the eggplant, corn and juices, squash, and chicken broth and bring to a simmer. Cook, stirring once or twice, until thick, about 10 minutes. Stir in the basil, remove the skillet from the heat, and let stand, covered, for 1 minute. Serve hot or at room temperature.

# Red Chile~Cheese Bread

**F**INE-TEXTURED, WITH AN ASTONISHINGLY BEAUTIFUL RED COLOR, this bread will become a favorite. Serve it with soup or stew, of course, but to see it at its best, try it toasted to make your favorite sandwich (try grilled chicken breast slathered with guacamole...*yes!*).

| | |
|---|---|
| 1 cup warm (105° to 115°F) water | About 4 cups unbleached all-purpose flour |
| 2 tablespoons honey | 1 tablespoon olive oil |
| 1 envelope dry yeast | 2 to 3 tablespoons yellow cornmeal |
| 1 cup Red Chile Purée (page 21) | 1 egg beaten with 1 tablespoon cold water |
| 1 tablespoon salt | 1/4 pound jalapeño Jack cheese, grated |
| 1 cup whole-wheat flour, preferably stone ground | |

In a large mixing bowl, stir together the water, honey, and yeast. Let stand until foamy, about 5 minutes. Stir in the chile purée and salt. Whisk in the whole-wheat flour. Stir in enough of the all-purpose flour (about 2 1/2 cups) to make a soft dough. Turn the dough out onto a well-floured work surface and knead for 5 minutes, incorporating additional flour to make a soft, supple dough; form into a ball. Coat a large bowl with the olive oil. Add the ball of dough and turn to oil it on all sides. Cover with a clean towel and let stand at room temperature until doubled in bulk, about 2 hours.

Punch down the dough and turn it out onto a lightly floured work surface. Knead until stiff, about 5 minutes. Return the dough to the bowl, cover, and let stand until doubled, about 2 hours.

Sprinkle a large baking sheet with the cornmeal. Punch down the dough and turn it out onto an unfloured work surface. Divide the dough in half; form each half into a round loaf. Set the loaves on the prepared baking sheet, spacing them well apart. Cover the loaves with a towel and let rise until doubled, about 45 minutes.

Position a rack in the middle of the oven and preheat to 400°F. Brush the loaves with the egg mixture, coating them several times. Set the baking sheet in the oven and bake for 15 minutes. Press the grated cheese on the tops of the loaves, dividing it evenly. Bake another 15 to 20 minutes, or until the cheese has melted and browned lightly and the loaves, when thumped on their bottoms, sound hollow. Cool the loaves on a rack to room temperature before cutting.

# Santa Fe Breakfast Potatoes and Eggs

SANTA FE IS A BREAKFAST LOVER'S PARADISE, WHERE THE PORTIONS ARE AS BIG AS THE WIDE-OPEN SPACES. Real Santa Feans never skip breakfast, especially when these home fries are served, topped with Jack cheese, poached eggs, and the cook's choice of either red or green chile sauce. Serve with corn bread, toast, or tortillas to sop with the chile sauce enriched with the golden egg yolk.

1 1/2 pounds (3 medium) red-skinned potatoes
1/2 stick (4 tablespoons) unsalted butter
2 cups coarsely chopped yellow onions
Salt
1/2 teaspoon freshly ground black pepper

6 ounces Monterey Jack cheese, grated
1 tablespoon white wine vinegar
8 large eggs
1 1/3 cups Green Chile Sauce (page 23) or Red Chile Gravy (page 22), heated to simmering

In a medium saucepan, cover the potatoes with cold water. Set over medium heat, bring to a boil, and cook until just tender, about 30 minutes. Drain and cool. Peel the potatoes if you wish and cut them into 1/2-inch cubes. *(The potatoes can be prepared up to 1 day ahead; cover and refrigerate.)*

In a large heavy skillet over medium heat, melt the butter. Add the onions, cover, and cook for 5 minutes. Uncover and cook, stirring occasionally, until lightly browned, about 5 minutes. Add the potatoes, season them with 1/2 teaspoon salt and the pepper, and cook, uncovered, stirring occasionally, until lightly browned, about 20 minutes. Scatter the cheese over the potatoes, cover the skillet, and remove from the heat. Let stand until the cheese is melted, about 1 minute.

Meanwhile, set a large skillet of water over medium heat and bring it to a simmer. Stir in the vinegar. One at a time, crack each egg into a small bowl, then slide the egg into the hot water. Regulate the heat to avoid an active boil, and use a slotted spoon to gently shape the eggs into tidy ovals. Cook until done to your liking, about 3 minutes for fairly soft eggs.

Spoon the potatoes into 4 bowls. With a slotted spoon, lift the eggs one at a time from the water, drain briefly, and then set 2 eggs atop each bowl of potatoes. Spoon one-fourth of the chile sauce over each portion and serve immediately.

# Green Chile ~ Corn Cakes

**C**ORN AND CHILES ARE ONE OF THE SOUTHWEST'S CLASSIC COMBINATIONS, right up there with Roy Rogers and Dale Evans. If you don't have fresh oregano, try basil, marjoram, or sage, but don't use dried herbs for these pancakes. They are *perfecto* served as a side dish for grilled meats, but you have to try them for breakfast some morning with grilled sausages or ham (leave out the herbs in that case, as they don't go so well with maple syrup).

²/₃ cup yellow cornmeal, preferably stone
    ground

²/₃ cup masa harina (or substitute
    additional cornmeal)

¼ cup unbleached all-purpose flour

1 tablespoon sugar

1 teaspoon salt

½ teaspoon baking powder

2 cups buttermilk

2 eggs, well beaten

2 long green chiles, roasted, peeled, and
    chopped (page 11), or ⅓ cup frozen
    chopped hot green chiles, thawed and
    drained

⅓ cup tender sweet corn kernels and
    juices, cut and scraped from
    1 medium ear

1 tablespoon minced fresh oregano

½ stick (4 tablespoons) unsalted butter,
    melted, plus butter for the griddle

In a large bowl, sift together the cornmeal, masa harina, flour, sugar, salt, and baking powder. In a medium bowl, whisk together the buttermilk, eggs, green chiles, corn and juices, and oregano. Add the buttermilk mixture to the dry ingredients and partially combine. Add the melted butter and stir until just combined; do not overmix.

Warm a pancake griddle over medium heat. Butter the griddle. Working in batches, drop the batter by ¼ cupfuls onto the heated griddle. Spread the batter into 5-inch rounds and cook about 3 minutes, or until puffed and golden brown. Turn the cakes and cook until lightly colored and cooked through, about 2 minutes. Serve immediately.

# Pineapple Sorbet with Serranos and Purple Basil

**N**OT A DESSERT SORBET, BUT A REFRESHING EXOTICA TO SERVE BETWEEN COURSES AT A FANCY DINNER or as a treat on a hot summer day with a glass of iced tea. The combination of pineapple, basil, and chiles is intriguing, with only the slightest impression of heat.

1 ½ cups water

1 cup plus 2 tablespoons sugar

3 fresh serranos, stemmed and cut into thin rounds

5 medium sprigs of purple basil or sweet basil

1 medium pineapple (about 2 pounds), peeled, cored, and cut into 1-inch chunks

¼ cup fresh lime juice

In a small saucepan, combine the water, sugar, and serranos. Set over medium heat and bring just to a simmer, stirring to dissolve the sugar. Remove from the heat, stir in the basil, and let stand, covered, until cool. Strain the syrup and discard the serranos and basil.

In a food processor, combine the pineapple and lime juice and process until smooth. Combine the pineapple purée and serrano syrup, cover, and refrigerate until very cold, at least 5 hours.

Transfer the chilled pineapple mixture to the canister of an ice cream maker and churn according to the manufacturer's directions. Cover the churned sorbet tightly and store in the freezer. *(The sorbet can be prepared up to 2 days ahead.)* Soften slightly in the refrigerator if necessary before serving.

# Tostaditas

MAKES A PILE OF CHIPS

IT'S PRETTY DARNED HARD TO FIND REALLY GOOD SUPERMARKET TORTILLA CHIPS, and since it's so easy to make your own great ones, I will often fry up my own tostaditas (the Mexican word for chips). Fry up a dozen tortillas for six to eight people (or more if you've invited me). A baked version, which reduces the amount of fat, is included.

*24 6-inch yellow or blue corn tortillas*      *Corn or peanut oil, for deep-frying*      *Salt*

Stack the tortillas together a few at a time and with a long sharp knife, cut them into 6 equal wedges. Spread the tortillas on the work surface for 15 or 20 minutes to dry them slightly.

In an electric deep-fryer or a medium heavy saucepan fitted with a frying thermometer and set over moderate heat, warm the oil to between 375° and 400°F. (The fryer or pan should be no more than half full.) Working in batches to avoid overcrowding the fryer, cook the tortilla wedges, stirring them once or twice, until they are crisp but not browned, about 1 minute. With a slotted spoon, transfer the tostaditas to paper towels to drain. Sprinkle them lightly with salt to taste.

Baked Tostaditas: Preheat the oven to 350°F. Spread the cut tortillas on an ungreased baking sheet. Spray lightly with nonstick vegetable oil spray. Bake for 6 minutes. Turn the tostaditas, spray the other side, and continue baking until they are golden and crisp, about 3 minutes.

# Crema

MAKES ABOUT 2 CUPS

**C**REMA IS THE TANGY MEXICAN EQUIVALENT TO THE FRENCH CRÈME FRAÎCHE, thick cream that is similar to our sour cream but won't separate if heated. If you are using crema in a cold dish, you can substitute sour cream, but it won't be quite as good.

*2 cups heavy cream, preferably not*
  *ultra-pasteurized*

*3 tablespoons cultured buttermilk*
  *or plain yogurt*

In a bowl, whisk together the heavy cream and buttermilk. Loosely cover and let stand at room temperature for 12 hours; the mixture will thicken and become acidic. Cover and refrigerate until using; the cream will thicken further and become more tart. It will keep for up to 10 days.

# Pot Beans and Then Refried Beans

**W**HENEVER I SMELL THE AROMA OF SIMMERING BEANS IN A SOUTHWESTERN KITCHEN, I know some good food isn't far behind. They can be served as a soupy side dish, then mashed and refried the next day as a starchier accompaniment, somewhat like Mexican mashed potatoes.

## Pot Beans

2 pounds dried pinto beans, picked over

3 quarts water

1 ½ cups chopped yellow onions

¼ pound (4 or 5 strips) thick-sliced
 smoky bacon, chopped

1 tablespoon unblended medium-hot
 powdered red chiles, preferably from
 Chimayo or Dixon, New Mexico

3 garlic cloves, peeled and chopped

Salt

In a large bowl, soak the beans in cold water for 15 minutes, changing the water 3 times.

In a large pot (tall rather than wide), combine the rinsed beans, 3 quarts of water, the onions, bacon, powdered chiles, and garlic. Bring to a simmer, then partially cover and cook, stirring occasionally, for 2 hours. Stir in 4 teaspoons salt and cook until the beans are very tender and their broth is very thick, another hour or more. Adjust the seasoning and serve immediately. *(The beans can be prepared several days in advance and will improve upon resting. Cool completely, cover, and refrigerate. Rewarm the beans over low heat, stirring often, until simmering.)*

## Refried Beans

2 tablespoons olive oil

6 cups leftover pot beans, with their liquid

Warm the oil in a large nonstick skillet over low heat. Add 1 cup of the beans with liquid and cook, mashing them roughly and stirring often, until thick, about 5 minutes. Repeat, adding beans and liquid 1 cup at a time. The beans are done when they are thick and creamy but not dry. Serve immediately. *(The beans can be refried a few hours in advance. Add the last cup of beans with liquid and immediately remove the skillet from the heat. Partially cover and hold at room temperature. Rewarm over low heat, mashing and stirring until thick and creamy.)*

# Mail-Order Sources

THE EL PASO CHILE COMPANY
909 Texas Avenue
El Paso, TX 79901
(915) 544-3434
Dried chiles, powdered chiles, gifts, autographed
cookbooks, other southwestern ingredients

BUENO FOODS
2001 4th Street S.W.
Albuquerque, NM 87102
(505) 243-2722
Dried chiles, powdered chiles, frozen chopped
green chiles, red chile pastes

CASADOS FARMS
P.O. Box 852
San Juan Pueblo, NM 87566
(505) 852-2433
Chiles, powdered chiles, other
southwestern ingredients

THE CHILE SHOP
109 East Water Street
Santa Fe, NM 87501
(505) 983-6080
Dried chiles and powdered chiles

COYOTE CAFE GENERAL STORE
132 West Water Street
Santa Fe, NM 87501
(800) 866-HOWL
Dried chiles, powdered chiles, and chile pastes

DEAN & DELUCA
560 Broadway
New York, NY 10012
(800) 221-7714
Fresh and dried chiles and powdered chiles

MELISSA'S BRAND/WORLD VARIETY PRODUCE
P.O. Box 21127
Los Angeles, CA 90021
(800) 468-7111
Fresh and dried chiles

MO HOTTA MO BETTA
P.O. Box 4136
San Luis Obispo, CA 93403
(800) 462-3220
Dried chiles, powdered chiles, fresh habaneros

NATIVE SEEDS/SEARCH
2509 North Campbell Avenue, #325
Tucson, AZ 85719
(520) 327-9123
Heirloom chile seeds

SEEDS OF CHANGE
1364 Rufina Circle, #5
Santa Fe, NM 87501
(505) 983-8956
Chile seeds

SHEPHERD'S GARDEN SEEDS
30 Irene Street
Torrington, CT 06790
(203) 482-3638
Chile seeds

# Index

sauce, 23
green pumpkin seed salsa, for grilled cilantro
   swordfish, 39
grilled:
   cilantro swordfish with green pumpkin
      seed salsa, 37-39
   pork tenderloins with chipotle-marmalade
      glaze, 45

**H**abanero chiles, 6, 32
hot and cold tequila, 16

**I**sland chicken and fruit kabobs with
   jalapeño-peanut sauce, 34-36

**J**alapeño chiles, 6, 32, 34-36
   Café Centrál's "tromped-on"
      marinated, 29
   croutons, for sweet red pepper soup, 25
   green pumpkin seed salsa, for grilled
      cilantro swordfish, 39
   hot and cold tequila, 16
   kitchen cinco five-chile salsa, 8
   -peanut sauce, for island chicken and
      fruit kabobs, 36
   risotto with Sonoma Dry Jack
      cheese, 26

**K**abobs, island chicken and fruit, with
   jalapeño-peanut sauce, 34-36
kitchen cinco five-chile salsa, 8

**L**ittle tostadas of salmon ceviche with
   serranos, 18

**M**arinated:
   jalapeños, Café Centrál's "tromped-on," 29
   spareribs Chimayo, 43
mulatto chiles, 6
   kitchen cinco five-chile salsa, 8

**N**ew Mexico chiles, 6
   from Chimayo, 15, 28
   crunchy sweet and spicy chile pecans, 15
   from Dixon, 15, 28
   kitchen cinco five-chile salsa, 8
   marinated spareribs Chimayo, 43
   pot beans, 58
   red chile purée, 21
   Red River Valley barbecue sauce, 28
   refried beans, 58

**P**ecans, crunchy sweet and spicy chile, 15
pineapple sorbet with serranos and
      pineapple basil, 54
poblano chiles, 6
   rellenos with smoky tomato sauce, 41-42
   and vegetable ragout, 46
pork tenderloins, grilled, with chipotle-
      marmalade glaze, 45
potatoes and eggs, Santa Fe breakfast, 50
pot beans, 58
pumpkin seed salsa, green, for grilled
      cilantro swordfish, 39
purée, red chile, 21

**R**agout, vegetable and poblano, 46
red chile:
   -cheese bread, 49
   gravy, 22
   purée, 21
red pepper soup with jalapeño croutons,
      sweet, 25
Red River Valley barbecue sauce, 28
refried beans, 58
rellenos, poblano, with smoky tomato
      sauce, 41-42
risotto, jalapeño, with Sonoma Dry Jack
      cheese, 26
ristras, 10